A TOM SAWYER COMPANION

An Autobiographical Guided Tour with Mark Twain

John D. Evans

UNIVERSITY
PRESS OF
AMERICA

Lanham • New York • London

Copyright © 1993 by
University Press of America®, Inc.
4720 Boston Way
Lanham, Maryland 20706

3 Henrietta Street
London WC2E 8LU England

Library of Congress Cataloging-in-Publication Data

Evans, John D.
A Tom Sawyer companion : an autobiographical guided tour with
Mark Twain / by John D. Evans.
p.   cm.
Includes bibliographical references and index.
1. Twain, Mark, 1835–1910. Adventures of Tom Sawyer.   2. Twain,
Mark, 1835–1910—Homes and haunts—Missouri—Hannibal.
3. Autobiographical fiction, American—History and criticism.
4. Adventure stories, American—History and criticism.   5. Authors,
American—19th century—Biography.   6. Literary landmarks—
Missouri—Hannibal.   7. Hannibal (Mo.) in literature.   I. Title.
PS1306.E95   1993   813'.4—dc20   92–45858 CIP

ISBN 0–8191–9059–4 (cloth : alk. paper)
ISBN 0–8191–9060–8 (pbk. : alk. paper)

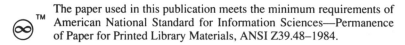

To my wife Deborah whose patience and encouragement

provided me with the time and energy

to devote to this project.

Acknowledgments

For permission to quote previously published material by Mark Twain, the author is indebted to the following publishers:

Mark Twain's Speeches, Copyrighted 1923, 1951, reprinted by permission of HarperCollins Publishers and The Mark Twain Company.

The Autobiography of Mark Twain, (Volumes I & II). Copyrighted 1927, 1940, 1959 by The Mark Twain Company. Copyright 1924, 1945, 1952 by Clara Clemens Samossoud. Copyrighted 1959 by Charles Neider. Reprinted by permission of HarperCollins Publishers and The Mark Twain Company.

The author is also indebted to the following people and organizations for their valuable assistance: Patricia Willis of the Beineke Rare Book and Manuscript Library at Yale University; Wendy Bowersock of the Harry Ransom Humanities Research Center of the University of Texas at Austin; Tom O'Sullivan of the Minnesota Historical Society in St. Paul; Henry Sweets, curator of The Mark Twain Museum in Hannibal, Missouri; Laura Goodale of the Mark Twain Project at the University of California; Robert C. Bogart, manager of the Mark Twain Cave; J. Hurley and Roberta Hagood, local historians at Hannibal, Missouri; and M'Lissa Kesterman of the Public Library of Cincinnati and Hamilton County.

A debt of gratitude is owed to the following individuals whose insights, advice and encouragement helped me more than they realize:, Drew C. Landry, Lola Shepherd, Albert V. Purdy, Ron Williams, and Michael W. Tieff.

Table of Contents

List of Photographs

Introduction

In his introduction to *The Adventures of Tom Sawyer*, Twain states, "Most of the adventures recorded in this book really occurred; one or two were experiences of my own, the rest those of boys who were schoolmates of mine." Like most authors, Twain wrote from personal experience, but, unlike many authors, he left behind a wealth of autobiographical material recording those personal experiences. His autobiography, letters, speeches, and notebooks contain many references to events similar to those presented in *Tom Sawyer*. On its simplest level, this book, in some measure, satisfies those whose curiosity is piqued by that simple admission by Twain.

On another level, this book may be used by those who wish to explore the creative process. Any work of fiction is more than just a few of the author's "experiences" strung together to form a plot. It is a melange of hopes, fears, aspirations, beliefs, misconceptions, habits, and observations which are filtered through the author's memory and reappear, perhaps somewhat altered, in the personalities and actions of his characters. It is no great surprise to those who know Mark Twain that Tom Sawyer is given a head full of curls—curls which "filled his life with bitterness." It is not important to the plot for Tom to have curly hair. He could have had long straight hair and the story would not suffer, but Tom Sawyer is, in part, Mark Twain, and Mark Twain understood the bitterness of curly hair. As a boy he struggled with his own "dense ruck of curly hair" trying desperately to wear it straight in the style of the day. In creating the character of Tom Sawyer, Twain used that small detail to round out Tom's personality, to make him a typical boy who is ashamed of his "effeminate" curls. It is a brush stroke in the portrait of Tom Sawyer that underscores his self-image as a bold, fearless adventurer. Details like this are important in the development of a character for in total they *become* the character, shaping his personality, directing his actions, and dictating his moods.

These parallels between reality and fiction can serve to show how Twain used personal experience as a springboard for his fiction, but that is not the true focus of this book. The focus is Twain and it is written for anyone who has read *The Adventures of Tom Sawyer* and enjoys Mark Twain as both a writer and a unique individual. Caution should be used by anyone who would try to analyze Twain through his autobiographical writings because, quite frankly, he told lies. In his *Advice to Youth*, Twain recommends that the young "be temperate in the use of this great art" until, through practice, they can make it "graceful and profitable." Twain was an undisputed master of the art. Like all great storytellers, he had a compulsion to make a good story better at the expense of truth. Perhaps Twain expresses it best through the words of Huckleberry Finn concerning *The Adventures of Tom Sawyer*: "That book was made by Mr. Mark Twain, and he told the truth, mainly. There was things which he stretched, but mainly he told the truth." Unfortunately for scholars, Twain was not averse to using "stretchers" in his autobiographical writings, and, although many events have been verified through newspapers and public records, the degree of Twain's involvement in them remains questionable. Another difficulty is that Twain's recollections of some experiences may have been dimmed by the passage of time. Twain was in his seventies when he recorded some of these events in his autobiography and with tongue-in-cheek he admitted: "When I was younger I could remember anything, whether it happened or not; but my faculties are decaying now, and soon I shall be so I cannot remember any but things that never happened." The purpose of this book, however, is neither to analyze *The Adventures of Tom Sawyer* nor to verify his autobiography but to present Mark Twain in the context of one of his great novels.

Each segment of this book is divided into three parts. The first is a running plot synopsis, in italics, which follows the chronology of events in *The Adventures of Tom Sawyer*. Editorial commentary is also given in italics when necessary to expand or clarify the material presented. The second part is a passage taken from the text of *Tom Sawyer*. These passages, in bold print, are the events or experiences that have their roots in reality. The third part is an autobiographical account, in plain text, which reveals those roots.

There are two approaches to reading Twain's autobiographical accounts. The first is to follow the method used by Twain's mother, Jane Lampton Clemens. Her formula for arriving at the facts was to "discount him 90 percent for embroidery" leaving behind "perfect and priceless truth." Unfortunately, she never shared with anyone exactly how she determined which "facts" were embroidery. The other approach is to take a more distant view. Instead of closely examining each statement for threads of truth, the reader can stand well back and take a more global view of Twain's autobiographical writings.

In his autobiography, Twain recounts a conversation he had with John Hay, then Secretary of State, concerning autobiographers who modify the truth: ". . . He will tell the truth in spite of himself, for his facts and his fictions will work loyally together for the protection of the reader; each fact and each fiction will be a dab of paint, each will fall in its right place, and together they will paint his portrait; not the portrait he thinks they are painting, but his real portrait, the inside of him, the soul of him, his character." Twain stated that his purpose in writing *Tom Sawyer* was "to pleasantly remind adults of what they were once themselves," and in doing so, he is also revealing to us what he once was himself. This book allows Twain to be Twain —"stretchers" and all—as he takes us back to the Hannibal of the 1840's to give us a guided tour of his boyhood. It gives the reader a "portrait" of Twain as the boy who grew up to be one of America's greatest writers. Whether fact or fiction, embellished truths or hazy memories, the words are pure Twain—sometimes nostalgic, sometimes humorous, but always captivating, always entertaining.

—John D. Evans
1992

1. Hand Me That Switch

In the opening scene of Tom Sawyer, *Aunt Polly searches for Tom and finds him hiding in a closet with the tell-tale evidence of jam on his face and hands. Angry at Tom for disobeying her about snitching jam for the "fortieth time," Aunt Polly takes a switch in hand to punish him.*

The switch hovered in the air—the peril was desperate—
"My! Look behind you, aunt!"
The old lady whirled round, and snatched her skirts out of danger. The lad fled, on the instant, scrambled up the high board fence, and disappeared over it.

—*Tom Sawyer*, **chapter 1**

Twain's daughter Susy began writing a biography of her father when she was thirteen. Hiding in her bedroom at night, she recorded impressions and incidents in the life of her father garnered from observations and conversations with other household members. Twain used these observations in his autobiography, keeping the precious words of his daughter intact and only making editorial comments to expand or clarify her impressions. Concerning the incident in which Tom Sawyer distracts Polly so he can escape punishment, Susy wrote: "Clara and I are sure papa played the trick on Grandma about the whipping, that is related in The Adventures of Tom Sawyer.*"*

Mark Twain's terse comment was:

Susy and Clara were quite right about that.

—*Autobiography*, Vol. II

Twain's mother, Jane Clemens. Courtesy Mark Twain Project, The Bancroft
Library.

2. Aunt Polly

After Tom escapes his punishment, Aunt Polly mutters to herself in a soliloquy that reveals her to be a simple soul who has the responsibility of raising her "own dead sister's boy." Her love for Tom is shown in her gentle laugh at his escape, and her deep concern for his upbringing is shown in her simple statement:

"I ain't doing my duty by that boy, and that's the Lord's truth, goodness knows. Spare the rod and spile the child, as the Good Book says. I'm a-laying up sin and suffering for us both, *I* know."

—*Tom Sawyer*, **chapter 1**

Twain used his mother, Jane Lampton Clemens, as a model for Aunt Polly. The following excerpt reveals the nature of her unique character and the changes Twain made in her for Tom Sawyer.

She never used large words, but she had a natural gift for making small ones do effective work. She lived to reach the neighborhood of ninety years and was capable with her tongue to the last—especially when a meanness or an injustice roused her spirit. She has come handy to me several times in my books, where she figures as Tom Sawyer's Aunt Polly. I fitted her out with a dialect and tried to think up other improvements for her, but did not find any . . . .

. . .She had a slender, small body, but a large heart—a heart so large that everybody's grief and everybody's joy found welcome in it, and hospitable accommodation. The greatest difference which I find between her and the rest of the people whom I have known, is this, and it is a remarkable one: those others felt a strong interest in a few things, whereas to the very day of her death she felt a strong interest in the whole world and everything and everybody in it . . . . Her interest in people and other animals was warm, personal, friendly . . . . One day in our village I saw a vicious devil of a Corsican, a common terror in the town, chasing his grown daughter past cautious male citizens with a heavy rope in his hand, and declaring he would wear it out on her. My mother spread her door wide to the refugee, and then, instead of closing and locking it after her, stood in it and stretched her arms across it, barring the way. The man swore, cursed, threatened her with his rope; but she did not flinch or show any sign of fear . . . . He and she were always good friends after that, for in her he had found a long—felt want—somebody who was not afraid of him.

One day in St. Louis she walked out into the street and greatly surprised a burly cartman who was beating his horse over the head with the butt of his heavy whip; for she took the whip away from him and then made such a persuasive appeal in behalf of the ignorant offending horse that he was tripped into saying he was to blame; and also into volunteering a promise which of course he couldn't keep, for he was not built that way—a promise that he wouldn't ever abuse a horse again . . . .

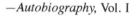

—*Autobiography,* Vol. I

Henry Clemens, two years younger than Twain, became Sid Sawyer.
Courtesy Mark Twain Project, The Bancroft Library.

3. A Thread of Evidence

After playing hooky as his Aunt Polly predicted he would, Tom appears at supper and steals sugar at every opportunity. Polly casually questions Tom about his day at school in an attempt to "trap him into damaging revealments." When this strategy fails, she asks to see his collar which she had sown shut to prevent him from swimming. Tom shows the collar, securely sewed, and Aunt Polly dismisses him.

She was half sorry her sagacity had miscarried, and half glad that Tom had stumbled into obedient conduct for once.

But Sid said:

"Well, now, if I didn't think you sewed his collar with white thread, but it's black."

"Why, I did sew it with white! Tom!"

But Tom did not wait for the rest.

—Tom Sawyer, **chapter 1**

My mother had a good deal of trouble with me, but I think she enjoyed it. She had none at all with my brother Henry, who was two years younger than I, and I think that the unbroken monotony of his goodness and truthfulness and obedience would have been a burden to her but for the relief which I furnished in the other direction. I was a tonic. I was valuable to her. I never thought of it before, but now I see it. I never knew Henry to do a vicious thing toward me, or toward anyone else—but he frequently did righteous ones that cost me as heavily. It was his duty to report me, when I needed reporting and neglected to do it myself, and he was very faithful in discharging that duty. He is Sid in *Tom Sawyer.* But Sid was not Henry. Henry was a very much finer and better boy than ever Sid was.

It was Henry who called my mother's attention to the fact that the thread with which she had sewed my collar together to keep me from going in swimming had changed color. My mother would not have discovered it but for that, and she was manifestly piqued when she recognized that that prominent bit of circumstantial evidence had escaped her sharp eye. That detail probably added a detail to my punishment. It is human. We generally visit our shortcomings on somebody else when there is a possible excuse for it—but no matter. I took it out of Henry.

—*Autobiography*, Vol. II

"Das Illustrirte Mississipithal" by Henry Lewis shows Hannibal during the 1840s. Courtesy the Minnesota Historical Society.

4. St. Petersburg

Tom makes another escape after he is caught playing hooky and runs into a new boy who has moved to town:

A stranger was before him—a boy a shade larger than himself. A newcomer of any age or sex was an impressive curiosity in the poor little shabby village of St. Petersburg.

—Tom Sawyer, **chapter 1**

Twain saw Hannibal as the ideal place for a boy to grow up. Thus Hannibal became St. Petersburg (St. Peter's burg), a little bit of heaven on earth. Twain visited his boyhood home twenty-nine years after leaving it to become a riverboat pilot, miner, reporter, and writer. His impression, after a generation of absence, was as follows:

The people of Hannibal are not more changed than is the town. It is no longer a village; it is a city, with a Mayor, and a council, and water-works, and probably a debt. It has fifteen thousand people, is a thriving and energetic place, and is paved like the rest of the West and South—where a well-paved street and sidewalk are things so seldom seen that one doubts them when he does see them. The customary half-dozen railways center in Hannibal now, and there is a depot, which cost a hundred thousand dollars. In my time the town had no specialty, and no commercial grandeur; the daily packet usually landed a passenger and bought a catfish, and took away another passenger and a hatful of freight; but now a huge commerce in lumber has grown up, and a large miscellaneous commerce is one of the results. A deal of money changes hands there now.

—Life on the Mississippi

5. Slaves and Slavery

Tom's misconduct of stealing jam, playing hooky, fighting, and coming home late finally gives Aunt Polly the resolve to turn Tom's Saturday into "captivity at hard labor." He is sentenced to whitewash "thirty yards of board fence nine feet high." Jim, a young slave, passes by with a bucket on his way to the town pump:

He remembered that there was company at the pump. White, mulatto, and Negro boys and girls were always there waiting their turns, resting, trading playthings, quarreling, fighting, skylarking.

—Tom Sawyer, **chapter 2**

The Missouri of Twain's youth was a slave-holding state, and, as a boy, Twain accepted slavery as a natural state of affairs. Later he would explore the moral issue of slavery in The Adventures of Huckleberry Finn, *but in* Tom Sawyer *he treated it as he had as a youth—it simply was not an issue.*

All the negroes were friends of ours, and with those of our own age we were in effect comrades. I say in effect, using the phrase as a modification. We were comrades, and yet not comrades; color and condition interposed a subtle line which both parties were conscious of and which rendered complete fusion impossible. We had a faithful and affectionate good friend, ally, and adviser in "Uncle Dan'l," a middle-aged slave whose head was the best one in the negro quarter, whose sympathies were wide and warm, and whose heart was honest and simple and knew no guile. He has served me well these many, many years. I have not seen him for more than half a century, and yet spiritually I have had his welcome company a good part of that time, and have staged him in books under his own name [*The American Claimant*] and as "Jim," and carted him all around—to Hannibal, down the Mississippi on a raft [*The Adventures of Huckleberry Finn*], and even across the Desert of Sahara in a balloon [*Tom Sawyer Abroad*]—and he has endured it all with the patience and friendliness and loyalty which were his birthright.

In my schoolboy days I had no aversion to slavery. I was not aware that was anything wrong about it. No one arraigned it in my hearing; the local papers said nothing against it; the local pulpit taught us that God approved it, that it was a holy thing, and that the doubter need only look in the Bible if he wished to settle his mind—and then the texts were read aloud to us to make the matter sure; if the slaves themselves had an aversion to slavery, they were wise and said nothing. In Hannibal we seldom saw a slave misused; on the farm never.

. . . .

However, there was nothing about the slavery of the Hannibal region to rouse one's dozing humane instincts to activity. It was the mild domestic slavery, not the brutal plantation article. Cruelties were very rare, and exceedingly and wholesomely unpopular. To separate and sell the members of a slave family to different masters was a thing not well liked by the people, and so it was not often done, except in the settling of estates. I have no recollection of ever seeing a slave auction in that town; but I am suspicious that that is because the thing was a common and commonplace spectacle, not an uncommon and impressive one. I vividly remember seeing a dozen black men and women chained to one another, once, and lying in a group on the pavement, awaiting shipment to the Southern slave market. Those were the saddest faces I have ever seen. Chained slaves could not have been a common sight, or this picture would not have made so strong and lasting an impression upon me.

The "nigger trader" was loathed by everybody. He was regarded as a sort of human devil who bought and conveyed poor helpless creatures to hell—for to our whites and blacks alike the Southern plantation was simply hell; no milder name could describe it. If the threat to sell an incorrigible slave "down the river" would not reform him, nothing would—his case was past cure.

It is commonly believed that an infallible effect of slavery was to make such as lived in its midst hard-hearted. I think it had no such effect—speaking in general terms. I think it stupefied everybody's humanity, as regarded the slave, but stopped there. There were no hard-hearted people in our town—I mean there were no more than would be found in any other town of the same size in any other country; and in my experience hard-hearted people are very rare everywhere.

—*Autobiography*, Vol. I

6. Big Missouri

Tom is not successful in getting Jim to whitewash the fence. As he is working, one of his friends, pretending to be a riverboat, arrives on the scene.

Ben Rogers hove in sight presently . . . . As he drew near, he slackened speed, took the middle of the street, leaned far over to starboard and rounded to ponderously and with laborious pomp and circumstance—for he was personating the *Big Missouri* . . . . He was boat and captain and engine bells combined . . . .

— Tom Sawyer, **chapter 2**

When I was a boy, there was but one permanent ambition among my comrades in our village on the west bank of the Mississippi River. That was to be a steamboatman. We had transient ambitions of other sorts, but they were only transient. When a circus came and went, it left us all burning to be clowns; the first minstrel show that ever came to our section left us all suffering to try that kind of life; now and then we had a hope that if we lived and were good, God would permit us to be pirates. These ambitions faded out, each in its turn; but the ambition to be a steamboatman always remained.

—Life on the Mississippi

7. A Well of Truth

In one of the most famous scenes in American literature, Tom convinces his friends that whitewashing a fence is play. He sells whitewashing privileges for a fortune in boyish treasures.[1] With the fence whitewashed with three coats, Tom presents himself before Aunt Polly to ask permission to go play. Polly does not believe Tom when he tells her that his job is finished:

"Tom, don't lie to me—I can't bear it." . . . She would have been content to find twenty percent of Tom's statement true.

—*Tom Sawyer*, **chapter 3**

When I was seven or eight or ten or twelve years old—along there—a neighbor said to her [Jane Clemens], "Do you ever believe anything that that boy says?" My mother said, "He is a wellspring of truth, but you can't bring up the whole well with one bucket"—and she added, "I know his average, therefore he never deceives me. I discount him 90 per cent for embroidery, and what is left is perfect and priceless truth, without a flaw in it anywhere."

—*Autobiography*, Vol. I

---

[1]On March 17, 1901, The New York Times reported on a speech given by Twain at a meeting of the New York City Male Teachers Association. During the course of his speech, Twain recounted incidents from his boyhood which later became part of his books. Concerning the whitewashing incident, the Times reported: "The fence whitewashing incident in 'Tom Sawyer,' he said, brought him in $4,000 in the end, when he never expected to get anything for teaching the other boys how to whitewash way back in 1849."

Mark Twain's boyhood home. Photograph by Deborah Rush Evans

8. Clodding Sid

Aunt Polly dismisses Tom for the day, praising him for his ability to work when he wants to. As he skips out of the house in his new freedom, he seizes a chance to get revenge on Sid for reminding Aunt Polly about the thread on his collar.

Then he skipped out, and saw Sid just starting up the outside stairway that led to the back rooms on the second floor. Clods were handy and the air was full of them in a twinkling.

—Tom Sawyer, **chapter 3**

There was a stairway outside the house, which led up to the rear part of the second story. One day Henry was sent on an errand, and he took a tin bucket along. I knew he would have to ascend those stairs, so I went up and locked the door on the inside, and came down into the garden, which had been newly plowed and was rich in choice, firm clods of black mold. I gathered a generous equipment of these and ambushed him. I waited till he had climbed the stair and was near the landing and couldn't escape. Then I bombarded him with clods, which he warded off with his tin bucket the best he could, but without much success, for I was a good marksman. The clods smashing against the weather-boarding fetched my mother out to see what was the matter, and I tried to explain that I was amusing Henry. Both of them were after me in a minute, but I knew the way over that high board fence and escaped for that time. After an hour or two, when I ventured back, there was no one around and I thought the incident was closed. But it was not so. Henry was ambushing me. With an unusually competent aim for him, he landed a stone on the side of my head which raised a bump there which felt like the Matterhorn. I carried it to my mother straightaway for sympathy, but she was not strongly moved. It seemed to be her idea that incidents like this would eventually reform me if I harvested enough of them. So the matter was only educational. I had had a sterner view of it than that before.

—Autobiography, Vol. II

Laura Hawkins lived in this house directly across the street from the Clemens's house on Hill St. She became Becky Thatcher in *The Adventures of Tom Sawyer*. Photograph by Deborah Rush Evans.

9. Childhood Sweethearts

Having gotten even with Sid, Tom runs off to play war with Jeff Thatcher. After the dead are counted and the prisoners exchanged, Tom turns to go home, but he stops when he notices a new girl:

As he was passing by the house where Jeff Thatcher lived, he saw a new girl in the garden . . . . A certain Amy Lawrence vanished out of his heart and left not even a memory of herself behind . . . .

—Tom Sawyer, **chapter 3**

In his autobiography, Twain looked back over sixty years to his sweethearts. Although Laura Hawkins, a girl who lived across the street from the Clemens's residence, was Twain's model for Becky Thatcher, this excerpt reveals how quickly Twain, like Tom, could fall in and out of love as a boy.

I recall Mary Miller. She was not my first sweetheart, but I think she was the first one that furnished me a broken heart. I fell in love with her when she was eighteen and I nine—but she scorned me, and I recognized that this was a cold world. I had not noticed that temperature before. I believe I was miserable as a grown man could be. But I think that this sorrow did not remain with me long. As I remember it, I soon transferred my worship to Artimisia Briggs, who was a year older than Mary Miller. When I revealed my passion to her she did not scoff at it. She did not make fun of it. She was very kind and gentle about it. But she was also firm, and said she did not want to be pestered by children.

—Autobiography, Vol. II

Laura Hawkins was Twain's model for Becky Thatcher

10. Broken Sugar Bowls

Tom is so absorbed with thoughts of his new girlfriend that he takes his scolding for clodding Sid and tries to steal sugar "under his aunt's very nose." When his knuckles get rapped, he protests that Sid is never punished for this crime. Polly explains that Sid doesn't torment her the way Tom does, and then she leaves the room.

Presently she stepped into the kitchen, and Sid, happy in his immunity, reached for the sugar bowl—a sort of glorying over Tom that was well-nigh unbearable. But Sid's fingers slipped and the bowl dropped and broke.

—Tom Sawyer, **chapter 3**

Henry never stole sugar. He took it openly from the bowl. His mother knew he wouldn't take sugar when she wasn't looking, but she had her doubts about me. Not exactly doubts, either. She knew very well I *would*. One day when she was not present Henry took sugar from her prized and precious old-English sugar bowl, which was an heirloom in the family—and he managed to break the bowl. It was the first time I had ever had a chance to tell anything on him, and I was inexpressibly glad. I told him I was going to tell on him, but he was not disturbed. When my mother came in and saw the bowl lying on the floor in fragments, she was speechless for a minute. I allowed that silence to work; I judged it would increase the effect. I was waiting for her to ask, "Who did that?"—so that I could fetch out my news. But it was an error of calculation. When she got through with her silence she didn't ask anything about it—she merely gave me a crack on the skull with her thimble that I felt all the way down to my heels. Then I broke out with my injured innocence, expecting to make her very sorry that she had punished the wrong one. I expected her to do something remorseful and pathetic. I told her that I was not the one—it was

Henry. But there was no upheaval. She said, without emotion: "It's all right. It isn't any matter. You deserve it for something you've done that I didn't know about; and if you haven't done it, why then you deserve it for something that you are going to do that I shan't hear about."

—*Autobiography,* Vol. II

This is Bear Creek today. The course of Bear Creek was altered when the railroad went through Hannibal in 1852, but Mark Twain's swimming hole may have looked much like this one. Photograph by Deborah Rush Evans.

11. Drowning

Tom wallows in self-pity after being wrongly accused of breaking his aunt's sugar bowl and looks for "desolate places that were in harmony with his spirit."

A log raft in the river invited him, and he seated himself on its outer edge and contemplated the dreary vastness of the stream, wishing, the while, that he could only be drowned, all at once and unconsciously, without undergoing the uncomfortable routine devised by nature.

—Tom Sawyer, **chapter 3**

Mark Twain was no stranger to that "uncomfortable routine devised by nature." By his own account, he narrowly escaped drowning several times in Bear Creek and in the Mississippi. In the episode that follows, Twain is rescued by an apprentice and a slave woman belonging to Mr. William F. Kercheval, the tailor. Twain, embittered by the deaths of his wife and daughter, later commented with grim humor, " . . . I can't feel either very kindly or forgivingly toward either that good apprentice boy or that good slave woman, for they saved my life."

One day when I was playing on a loose log which I supposed was attached to a raft—but wasn't—it tilted me into Bear Creek. And when I had been under water twice and was coming up for the third and fatal descent, my fingers appeared above the water and that slave woman seized them and pulled me out. Within a week I was in again, and that apprentice had to come along just at the wrong time, and he plunged in and dived, pawed around on the bottom and found me, and dragged me out, emptied the water out of me, and I was saved again. I was drowned seven times after that before I learned to swim—once in Bear Creek and six times in the Mississippi. I do not now know who the people were who interfered with the intentions of a Providence wiser than themselves, but I hold a grudge against them yet.

—Autobiography, Vol. II

This photograph of Mark Twain reveals his "dense ruck of short curls." Courtesy Mark Twain Project, The Bancroft Library.

12. Curls

When Sunday comes, Tom participates in family worship, studies his lessons, and, with the help of his cousin Mary, he is washed and dressed, and his "saturated hair was neatly brushed, and its short curls wrought into a dainty and symmetrical general effect."

He privately smoothed out the curls, with labor and difficulty, and plastered his hair close down to his head; for he held curls to be effeminate, and his own filled his life with bitterness.

— Tom Sawyer, **chapter 4**

In the above passage, Mark Twain allows his personal frustrations with his hair to shine through. In the following passage, he explains why:

In that day it was a great thing among the boys to have hair of so flexible a sort that it could be flung back . . . with a flirt of the head. George RoBards was the envy of us all. For there was no hair among us that was so competent for this exhibition as his. My hair was a dense ruck of short curls, and so was my brother Henry's. We tried all kinds of devices to get these crooks straightened out so that they would flirt, but we never succeeded. Sometimes by soaking our heads and then combing and brushing our hair down tight and flat to our skulls, we could get it straight, temporarily, and this gave us a comforting moment of joy. But the first time we gave it a flirt it all shriveled into curls again and our happiness was gone.

—Autobiography, Vol. II

13. Three Thousand Verses

Before Sunday school, Tom trades his wealth gained by selling whitewashing privileges for tickets of various colors. These tickets, proof that the holder has memorized Bible verses, can be redeemed for "a very plainly bound Bible."

. . . Mary had acquired two Bibles in this way—it was the patient work of two years—and a boy of German parentage had won four or five. He once recited three thousand verses without stopping; but the strain upon his mental faculties was too great, and he was little better than an idiot from that day forth . . . .

— Tom Sawyer, **chapter 4**

In A Scrap of Curious History, *Twain mentions Ed Smith, a nineteen year old printer's apprentice, as the boy who could recite three thousand verses. The Dutchy in the following passage is most likely the same person. Dutchy did not lose his wits as a result of his feat, but tragedy struck soon after his accomplishment and furnished Mark Twain with material for this satirical comment.*

Dutchy belonged to our Sunday-school. He was a German lad who did not know enough to come in out of the rain; but he was exasperatingly good, and had a prodigious memory. One Sunday he made himself the envy of all the youth and the talk of the admiring village, by reciting three thousand verses of Scripture without missing a word: then he went off the very next day and got drowned.

—Life on the Mississippi

14. Sunday School Tickets

When the Sunday school is visited by Judge Thatcher, everyone shows off. Mr. Walters, the superintendent, would give anything to be able to "exhibit a prodigy" and deliver "a Bible prize," but no one has earned enough tickets.

And now at this moment, when hope was dead, Tom Sawyer came forward with nine yellow tickets, nine red tickets, and ten blue ones, and demanded a Bible.

—Tom Sawyer, **chapter 4**

In about 1865, Mark Twain wrote "The Story of the Good Little Boy," and "The Story of the Bad Little Boy." These two short sketches satirized the heavy-handed moralizing of Thomas Bailey Aldrich's <u>The Story of a Bad Boy</u>. *Twain objected to the literature of his day in which all bad boys came to no good and all good boys were rewarded in life. Twain recognized that this was not realistic, especially in light of his own youth and later success. In* <u>The Adventures of Tom Sawyer</u>, *Twain explored this issue even further having Tom become a hero again and again in spite of his mischief.*

The foundation for Twain's distaste for moralistic stories is revealed in the following passage:

. . . My Methodist Sunday-school teacher in the earliest days . . . had one distinction which I envied him: He was a very kindly and considerate Sunday school teacher, and patient and compassionate, so he was the favorite teacher with us little chaps. In that school they had slender oblong pasteboard blue tickets, each with a verse from the Testament printed on it, and you could get a blue ticket by reciting two verses. By reciting five verses you could get three blue tickets, and you could trade these at the bookcase and borrow a book for a week. I was under Mr. Richmond's spiritual care every now and then for two or three years, and he was never hard upon me. I always recited the same five verses every Sunday [Matt. 25:1-5]. He was always satisfied with the performance. He never seemed to notice that these were the same five foolish virgins that he had been hearing about every Sunday for months. I always got my tickets and exchanged them for a book. They were pretty dreary books, for there was not a bad boy in the entire bookcase. They were *all* good boys and good girls and drearily uninteresting, but they were better society than none, and I was glad to have their company and disapprove of it.

—*Autobiography,* Vol. II

15. The Model Boy

Tom wins his Bible prize and is asked by Judge Thatcher to name the first two disciples. After embarrassing everyone with his answer of "David and Goliath," Tom attends church. The congregation enters the building and files down the aisle to their accustomed places.

. . . And last of all came the Model Boy, Willie Mufferson, taking as heedful care of his mother as if she were cut glass. He always brought his mother to church, and was the pride of all the matrons. The boys all hated him, he was so good.

—Tom Sawyer, **chapter 5**

The Model Boy of my time—we never had but the one—was perfect: perfect in manners, perfect in dress, perfect in conduct, perfect in filial piety, perfect in exterior godliness; but at the bottom, he was a prig; and as for contents of his skull, they could have changed place with the contents of a pie, and nobody would have been the worse off for it but the pie. This fellow's reproachlessness was a standing reproach to every lad in the village. He was the admiration of all the mothers, and the detestation of all their sons.

—Life on the Mississippi

. . . Theodore [Dawson] . . . was as good as he could be. In fact he was inordinately good, extravagantly good, offensively good, detestably good—and he had pop-eyes—and I would have drowned him if I had had a chance.

—Autobiography, Vol. II

This is an early Hannibal school identified as one attended by Mark Twain and Laura Hawkins. Courtesy the Mark Twain Museum.

16. Hooky

Tom suffers an eternity during the church service but finds some satisfaction when his pinchbug adds "a bit of variety in it."

His weekend comes to a close, and now he faces "another week's slow suffering in school."

Monday morning found Tom miserable . . . because it began another week's slow suffering in school . . . .   Presently it occurred to him that he wished he was sick; then he could stay home from school . . . so he fell to groaning with considerable spirit . . . .

Sid flew downstairs and said:

"Oh, Aunt Polly, come! Tom's dying!"

—Tom Sawyer, **chapter 6**

Once again, Susy Clemens' biography of her father gives us some insight into Twain's school attendance, and again Twain adds his own terse comment.

From Susy's biography:

And we know papa played "Hookey" all the time.   And how readily would papa pretend to be dying so as not to have to go to school!

These revelations and exposures are searching, but they are just. If I am as transparent to other people as I was to Susy, I have wasted much effort in this life.

—Autobiography, Vol. II

17. Dentistry

Tom canvasses his system searching for some ailment that would keep him home from school.

Suddenly he discovered something. One of his upper front teeth was loose. This was lucky; he was about to begin to groan as a "starter," as he called it, when it occurred to him that if he came into court with that argument, his aunt would pull it out, and that would hurt.

— *Tom Sawyer*, **chapter 6**

There were no dentists. When teeth became touched with decay or were otherwise ailing, the doctor knew of but one thing to do—he fetched out his tongs and dragged them out. If the jaw remained, it was not his fault.

—*Autobiography,* Vol. I

Tom Blankenship lived with his father in this wooden structure in the foreground. It was razed after a fire. Courtesy Mark Twain Museum.

18. The Homeless Outcast

Tom's scheme to stay home from school fails. Aunt Polly pulls the tooth and sends Tom off to school. On the way, he is delayed when he meets Huckleberry Finn.

Shortly Tom came upon the juvenile pariah of the village, Huckleberry Finn, son of the town drunkard. Huckleberry was cordially hated and dreaded by all the mothers of the town, because he was idle and lawless and vulgar and bad—and because all their children admired him so . . . .

— Tom Sawyer, **chapter 6**

"Huckleberry Finn" was Tom Blankenship. Tom's father was at one time Town Drunkard, an exceedingly well-defined and unofficial office of those days . . . . I have drawn Tom Blankenship exactly as he was. He was ignorant, unwashed, insufficiently fed; but he had as good a heart as ever any boy had. His liberties were totally unrestricted. He was the only really independent person—man or boy—in the community, and by consequence he was envied by all the rest of us. We liked him; we enjoyed his society. And as his society was forbidden us by our parents, the prohibition trebled and quadrupled its value, and therefore we sought and got more of his society than that of any other boy's.

—Autobiography, Vol. II

19. Becky Thatcher

Tom and Huck make plans to cure warts at the graveyard later that night, and Huck trades his tick for Tom's tooth. Tom races to school, and as a punishment for being late, he is forced to sit with the "new girl," Becky Thatcher.

Presently the boy began to steal furtive glances at the girl.   She observed it, "made a mouth" at him and gave him the back of her head for the space of a minute.   When she cautiously faced around again, a peach lay before her.   She thrust it away.   Tom gently put it back.   She thrust it away again, but with less animosity.   Tom patiently returned it to its place.   Then she let it remain.

— *Tom Sawyer*, **chapter 6**

On October 9, 1908, Twain wrote to a twelve year old Denver girl whom he had met in Bermuda. He asked her if she liked romances and then proceeded to tell about "the very first sweetheart I ever had." He was referring to Annie Laurie Hawkins, or more familiarly, Laura Hawkins. (SCH)

She was 5 years old, and I the same. I had an apple, and I fell in love with her and gave her the core. I remember it perfectly well and exactly the place where it happened, and what kind of day it was. She figures in "Tom Sawyer" as "Becky Thatcher." Or maybe in "Huck Finn" — anyway it is in one of those books.

—Letter to Margaret Blackmer
October 9, 1908 (SCH)

20. Spelling

Tom impresses Becky with his art work, and they make arrangements to eat lunch together at noon. Tom is so preoccupied with his new girl friend that he cannot concentrate on his studies.

As the school quieted down Tom made an honest effort to study, but the turmoil within was too great. In turn he took his place in the reading class and made a botch of it . . . then in the spelling class, and got "turned down," by a succession of mere baby words, till he brought up at the foot and yielded up the pewter medal which he had worn with ostentation for months.

—Tom Sawyer, **chapter 6**

. . . I have had an aversion to good spelling for sixty years and more, merely for the reason that when I was a boy there was not a thing I could do creditably except spell according to the book. It was a poor and mean distinction, and I early learned to disenjoy it. I suppose that this is because the ability to spell correctly is a talent, not an acquirement. There is some dignity about an acquirement, because it is a product of your own labor. It is wages earned, whereas to be able to do a thing merely by the grace of God, and not by your own effort, transfers the distinction to our heavenly home—where possibly it is a matter of pride and satisfaction, but leaves you naked and bankrupt. . . .

. . . When I was a schoolboy, sixty years ago, we had two prizes in our school. One was for good spelling, the other for amiability. These things were thin, smooth, silver disks, about the size of a dollar. Upon the one was engraved in flowing Italian script the words "Good Spelling," on the other was engraved the word "Amiability." The holders of these prizes hung them about the neck with a string—and those holders were the envy of the whole school. There wasn't a pupil that wouldn't have given a leg for the privilege of wearing one of them a week, but no pupil ever got a chance except John RoBards and me. John RoBards was eternally and indestructibly amiable. I may even say devilishly amiable; fiendishly amiable; exasperatingly amiable. That was the sort of feeling that we had about that quality of his. So he always wore the amiability medal. I always wore the other medal. The word "always" is a trifle too strong. We lost the medals several times.

It was because they became so monotonous. We needed a change—therefore several times we traded medals. It was a satisfaction to John RoBards to *seem* to be a good speller—which he wasn't. And it was a satisfaction to me to seem to be amiable, for a change. But of course these changes could not long endure—for some schoolmate or other would presently notice what had been happening, and that schoolmate would not have been human if he had lost any time in reporting this treason. The teacher took the medals away from us at once, of course—and we always had them back again before Friday night. If we lost the medals Monday morning, John's amiability was at the top of the list Friday afternoon when the teacher came to square up the week's account. The Friday-afternoon session always closed with "spell down." Being in disgrace, I necessarily started at the foot of my division of spellers, but I always slaughtered both divisions and stood alone with the medal around my neck when the campaign was finished. I *did* miss on a word once, just at the end of one of these conflicts, and so lost the medal. I left the first *r* out of February—but that was to accommodate a sweetheart[2]. My passion was so strong just at that time that I would have left out the whole alphabet if the word had contained it.

—*Autobiography*, Vol. II

---

[2]According to Paine's biography of Twain, this sweetheart was Laura Hawkins, the model for Becky Thatcher. (MTB)

21. School Days

Tom writes "I love you" on his slate, and "a little scuffle" ensues as Becky tries to read it. The master, Mr. Dobbins, moves Tom back to his own seat next to Joe Harper. Tom tries to study, but his mind wanders. He soon gives up and is oppressed by "the sleepiest of sleepy days."

The drowsing murmur of the five and twenty studying scholars soothed the soul like the spell that is in the murmur of bees. Away off in the flaming sunshine, Cardiff Hill lifted its soft green sides through a shimmering veil of heat, tinted with the purple of distance . . . ."

—Tom Sawyer, **chapter 7**

I remember Dawson's schoolhouse perfectly. If I wanted to describe it I could save myself the trouble by conveying the description of it to these pages from *Tom Sawyer*. I can remember the drowsy and inviting summer sounds that used to float in through the open windows from that distant boy-Paradise, Cardiff Hill, and mingle with the murmurs of the studying pupils and make them the more dreary by contrast. I remember Andy Fuqua, the oldest pupil—a man of twenty-five. I remember the youngest pupil, Nannie Owsley, a child of seven. I remember George RoBards, eighteen or twenty years old, the only pupil who studied Latin. I remember vaguely the rest of the twenty-five boys and girls. I remember Mr. Dawson very well . . . . In that school we were all about on an equality, and, so far as I remember, the passion of envy had no place in our hearts, except in the case of Arch Fuqua—the other's brother. Of course we all went barefoot in the summertime. Arch Fuqua was about my own age—ten or eleven. In the winter we could stand him, because he wore shoes then, and his great gift was hidden from our sight and we were enabled to forget it. But in the summertime he was a bitterness to us. He was our envy, for he could double back his big toe and let it fly and you could hear it snap thirty yards. There was not another boy in the school that could approach his feat. He had not a rival as regards a physical distinction—except in Theodore Eddy, who could work his ears like a horse. But he was no real rival, because you couldn't hear him work his ears; so all the advantage lay with Arch Fuqua.

And there was Mary Lacy. She was a schoolmate. But she also was out of my class because of her advanced age. She was pretty wild and determined and independent. She was ungovernable, and considered incorrigible. But that was all a mistake. She married, and at once settled down and became in all ways a model matron and was as highly respected as any matron in the town. Four years ago she was still living, and had been married fifty years.

Jimmie McDaniel was another schoolmate. His age and mine about tallied. His father kept the candy shop and was the most envied little chap in the town—after Tom Blankenship—for, although we never saw him eating candy, we supposed that it was, nevertheless, his ordinary diet. He pretended that he never ate it, didn't care for it because there was nothing forbidden about it—there was plenty of it and he could have as much of it as he wanted. Still, there was circumstantial evidence that suggested that he only scorned candy in public to show off, for he had the worst teeth in town.

—Autobiography, Vol. II

22. Tick-Running

"To pass the dreary time," Tom gets out his tick and places it upon his slate. He and Joe improvise a game in which each boy tries to keep the tick from crossing a line drawn down the middle of the slate.

The tick escaped from Tom, presently, and crossed the equator. Joe harassed him awhile and then he got away and crossed back again. This change of base occurred often. While one boy was worrying the tick with absorbing interest, the other would look on with interest as strong, the two heads bowed together over the slate and the two souls dead to all things else.

—*Tom Sawyer*, **chapter 7**

The incident of tick-running, including the teacher's unnoticed appearance behind the absorbed boys, was taken directly from his boyhood and deposited in fiction. In "Boy's Manuscript," an early version of <u>Tom Sawyer</u>, *Twain made a notation: "Every detail of the above incident is strictly true, as I have excellent reason to remember." Another autobiographical reference to this incident is found in a letter to Will Bowen, Twain's boyhood friend and model for Joe Harper.* (SCH)

I have been thinking of school-days at Dawson's, & trying to recall the old faces of that ancient time—but I cannot place them very well—they have faded out of my treacherous memory, for the most part, & passed away. But I still remember the louse you bought of poor Arch Fuqua. I told about that at a Congressional dinner in Washington the other day, & Lord, how those thieves laughed! It *was* a gorgeous old reminiscence. I just expect I shall publish it yet, some day.

—Letter to Will Bowen,
January 25, 1868,
New York, N. Y. (SCH)

23. A Pirate Bold To Be

*During the noon recess, Tom gets engaged to Becky who is angered when
Tom unwittingly reveals that he was already engaged to Amy Lawrence. When she
rebuffs his "chiefest jewel," a brass knob, as a peace offering, Tom runs away "to
return to school no more that day." He fantasizes about turning his back on this life
and returning at some future date covered with glory.*

He would be a pirate! That was it! <u>Now</u> his future lay plain before
him, and glowing with unimaginable splendor. How his name would
fill the world, and make people shudder! How gloriously he would go
plowing the dancing seas . . . . And at the zenith of his fame, how he
would suddenly appear at the old village and stalk into church . . . and
hear . . . the whisperings, "It's Tom Sawyer the Pirate!—The Black
Avenger of the Spanish Main!"

—Tom Sawyer, **chapter 8**

All that sentimentality and romance among young folk seem puerile, now, but
when one examines it and compares it with the ideals of to-day, it was the preferable
thing. It was soft, sappy, melancholy; but money had no place in it. To get rich was
no one's ambition—it was not in any young person's thoughts. The heroes of these
young people—even the pirates—were moved by lofty impulses: they waded in
blood, in the distant fields of war and adventure and upon the pirate deck, to rescue
the helpless, not to take the money: they spent their blood and made their self-
sacrifices for "honor's" sake, not to capture a giant fortune; they married for love, not
for money and position. It was an intensely sentimental age, but it took no sordid
form.

—Villagers of 1840-3 (HHT)

Cardiff Hill (Holliday's Hill) rises above Hannibal to the north. The lighthouse was erected in 1935 to commemorate the centennial of Twain's Birth. Photograph by Deborah Rush Evans.

24. Robin Hood

Tom begins his career as pirate by gathering his resources together. He unearths a small pine shingle treasure house in which he expects to find his lost marbles. According to a superstition, a marble buried with certain incantations will attract every marble ever lost. When this fails, Tom consults a doodlebug to satisfy his suspicion that a witch has interfered. Further experiments are interrupted by a trumpet blast that "came faintly down the green aisles of the forest."

Tom flung off his jacket and trousers, turned a suspender into a belt, raked away some brush behind the rotten log, disclosing a rude bow and arrow, a lath sword and a tin trumpet, and in a moment had seized these things and bounded away, barelegged, with fluttering shirt.

— *Tom Sawyer*, chapter 8

. . . We used to undress & play Robin Hood in our shirt-tails, with lath swords, in the woods on Halliday's Hill on those long summer days.

—Letter to Will Bowen
February 6, 1870
Buffalo, N. Y. (MTLWB)

The Old Baptist Cemetery on a hill north of town is the graveyard of Twain's boyhood. There are no recorded incidents of grave robbery. Photograph by Deborah Rush Evans.

25. Death and Violence

On Monday night, as planned, Tom and Huck venture into the graveyard with Huck's dead cat. Their plan to cure warts at Hoss Williams' grave is interrupted by three grave robbers. Dr. Robinson, who wants to examine Hoss Williams' body, gets into a fight with Injun Joe over his demand for more pay. Muff Potter joins the fight and grabs the young doctor.

All at once the doctor flung himself free, seized the heavy head-board of Williams' grave and felled Potter to the earth with it—and in the same instant the half-breed saw his chance and drove the knife to the hilt in the young man's breast.

—Tom Sawyer, **chapter 9**

It has been suggested that Twain borrowed this graveyard scene from his reading of Charles Dickens' A Tale of Two Cities, *and that might be so. Nevertheless, as a young boy, Twain saw enough violence to draw upon his own experience to furnish the images of Dr. Robinson falling upon Muff Potter and "flooding him with his blood."*

All within the space of a couple of years we had two or three . . . tragedies, and I had the ill luck to be too near by, on each occasion. There was a slave man who was struck down with a chunk of slag for some small offense: I saw him die. And the young California immigrant who was stabbed with a bowie knife by a drunken comrade; I saw the red life gush from his breast. And the case of the rowdy young brothers and their harmless old uncle: one of them held the old man down with his knees on his breast while the other one tried repeatedly to kill him with an Allen revolver which wouldn't go off. I happened along just then, of course.

—Autobiography, Vol. I

26. A Guilty Conscience

Tom and Huck flee into the night and take an oath "to keep mum." They are unaware that Injun Joe has framed Potter. By the time they learn of Joe's treachery, Potter is jailed for murder and their oath prevents them from speaking up in his defense. To ease their consciences, the boys visit Muff's jail window.

The boys did as they had often done before—went to the cell grating and gave Potter some tobacco and matches . . . . His gratitude for their gifts had always smote their consciences before—it cut deeper than ever, this time.

—Tom Sawyer, **chapter 23**

As a boy, Mark Twain carried a heavy burden of guilt that resulted from a gift of some matches. That gift, to a poor unfortunate tramp, caused him enough anguish to supply him with material to draw upon in creating the dilemma in which Tom finds himself: keeping a dreadful secret at the expense of the life of an innocent man held in jail. Twain recalls his own "fearful secret and gnawing conscience" in the following passage:

The slaughter-house is gone from the mouth of Bear Creek and so is the small jail (or "calaboose") which once stood in its neighborhood. A citizen asked, "Do you remember when Jimmy Finn, the town drunkard, was burned to death in the calaboose?"

Observe, now, how history becomes defiled, through lapse of time and the help of the bad memories of men. Jimmy Finn was not burned in the calaboose, but died a natural death in a tan vat, of a combination of delirium tremens and spontaneous combustion. When I say natural death, I mean it was a natural death for Jimmy Finn to die. The calaboose victim was not a citizen; he was a poor stranger, a harmless, whisky-sodden tramp. I know more about his case than anybody else; I knew too much of it, in that bygone day, to relish speaking of it. That tramp was wandering about the streets one chilly evening, with a pipe in his mouth, and begging for a match; he got neither matches nor courtesy; on the contrary, a troop of bad little boys followed him around and amused themselves with nagging and annoying him. I assisted; but at last, some appeal which the wayfarer made for forbearance accompanying it with a pathetic reference to his forlorn and friendless condition, touched such sense of shame and remnant of right feeling as were left in me, and I went away and got him some matches . . . . An hour or two afterward the man was arrested and locked up in the calaboose by the marshal—large name for a constable, but that was his title. At two in the morning, the church-bells rang for fire, and everybody turned out, of course I with the rest. The tramp had used his matches disastrously; he had set his straw bed on fire, and the oaken sheathing of the room had caught. When I reached the ground, two hundred men, women, and children stood massed together, transfixed with horror, and staring at the grated windows of the jail. Behind the iron bars, and tugging frantically at them, and screaming for help, stood the tramp; he seemed like a black object set against a sun, so white and intense was the light at his back. That marshal could not be found, and he had the only key. A batteringram was quickly improvised, and the thunder of its blows upon the door had so encouraging a sound that the spectators broke into wild cheering, and believed the merciful battle won. But it was not so. The timbers were too strong; they did not yield. It was said that the man's death-grip still held fast to the bars after he was dead; and that in this position the fires wrapped him about and consumed him. As to this, I do not know. What was seen, after I recognized the face that was pleading through the bars, was seen by others, not by me.

I saw that face, so situated, every night for a long time afterward; and I believed myself as guilty of the man's death as if I had given him the matches purposely that he might burn himself up with them. I had not a doubt that I should be hanged if my connection with this tragedy were found out. The happenings and the impressions of that time are burned into my memory, and the study of them entertains me as much now as they themselves distressed me then. If anybody spoke of that grisly matter, I was all ears in a moment, and alert to hear what might be said, for I was always dreading and expecting to find out that I was suspected; and so fine and so delicate was the perception of my guilty conscience that it often detected suspicion in the most purposeless remarks, and in looks, gestures, glances of the eye, which had no significance, but which sent me shivering away in a panic of fright, just the same. And how sick it made me when somebody dropped, howsoever carelessly and barren of intent, the remark that "murder will out!" For a boy of ten years, I was carrying a pretty weighty cargo.

—Life on the Mississippi

27. Keeping Mum

Tom's fearful secret and gnawing conscience disturbed his sleep for as much as a week after this; and at breakfast one morning Sid said:

"Tom, you pitch around and talk in your sleep so much that you keep me awake half the time."

—*Tom Sawyer,* chapter 11

In this continuation of the incident of the tramp who burned himself up, Mark Twain reveals how that "weighty cargo" affected his sleep.

All this time I was blessedly forgetting one thing—the fact that I was an inveterate talker in my sleep. But one night I awoke and found my bed-mate—my younger brother—sitting up in bed and contemplating me by the light of the moon. I said:

"What is the matter?"

"You talk so much I can't sleep."

I came to a sitting posture in an instant, with my kidneys in my throat and my hair on end.

"What did I say? Quick—out with it—what did I say?"

"Nothing much."

"It's a lie—you know everything!"

"Everything about what?"

"You know well enough. About *that.*"

"About *what?* I don't know what you are talking about. I think you are sick or crazy or something. But anyway, you're awake, and I'll get to sleep while I've got a chance."

He fell asleep and I lay there in a cold sweat, turning this new terror over in the whirling chaos which did duty as my mind. The burden of my thought was, how much did I divulge? How much does he know? What a distress is this uncertainty! But by and by I evolved an idea—I would wake my brother and probe him with a supposititious case. I shook him up, and said:

"Suppose a man should come to you drunk—"

"This is foolish—I never get drunk."

"I don't mean you, idiot—I mean the man. Suppose a man should come to you drunk, and borrow a knife, or a tomahawk, or a pistol, and you forgot to tell him it was loaded, and—"

"How could you load a tomahawk?"

"I don't mean the tomahawk, and I didn't *say* the tomahawk; I said the pistol. Now, don't you keep breaking in that way, because this is serious. There's been a man killed."

"What! In this town?"

"Yes, in this town."

"Well, go on—I won't say a single word."

"Well, then, suppose you forgot to tell him to be careful with it, because it was loaded, and he went off and shot himself with that pistol—fooling with it, you know, and probably doing it by accident, being drunk. Well, would it be murder?"

"No—suicide."

"No, no! I don't mean *his* act, I mean yours. Would you be a murderer for letting him have that pistol?"

After deep thought came this answer:

"Well, I should think I was guilty of something—maybe murder—yes, probably murder, but I don't quite know."

This made me very uncomfortable. However, it was not a decisive verdict. I should have to set out the real case—there seemed to be no other way. But I would do it cautiously, and keep a watch out for suspicious effects. I said:

"I was supposing a case, but I am coming to the real one now. Do you know how the man came to be burned up in the calaboose?"

"No."

"Haven't you the least idea?"

"Not the least."

"Wish you may die in your tracks if you have?"

"Yes, wish I may die in my tracks."

"Well, the way of it was this. The man wanted some matches to light his pipe. A boy got him some. The man set fire to the calaboose with those very matches, and burnt himself up."

"Is that so?"

"Yes, it is. Now, is that boy a murderer, do you think ?"

"Let me see. The man was drunk?"

"Yes, he was drunk."

"Very drunk?"

"Yes."

"And the boy knew it?"

"Yes, he knew it."

There was a long pause. Then came this heavy verdict:

"If the man was drunk, and the boy knew it, the boy murdered that man. This is certain."

Faint, sickening sensations crept along all the fibers of my body, and I seemed to know how a person feels who hears his death-sentence pronounced from the bench. I waited to hear what my brother would say next. I believed I knew what it would be, and I was right. He said:

"I know the boy."

I had nothing to say; so I said nothing. I simply shuddered. Then he added:

"Yes, before you got half through telling about the thing, I knew perfectly well who the boy was; it was Ben Coontz !"

I came out of my collapse as one who rises from the dead. I said, with admiration:

"Why, how in the world did you ever guess it?"

"You told me in your sleep."

I said to myself, "How splendid that is! This is a habit which must be cultivated."

My brother rattled innocently on:

"When you were talking in your sleep, you kept mumbling something about 'matches,' which I couldn't make anything out of; but just now, when you began to tell me about the man and the calaboose and the matches, I remembered that in your sleep you mentioned Ben Coontz two or three times; so I put this and that together, you see, and right away I knew it was Ben that burnt that man up."

I praised his sagacity effusively. Presently he asked:

"Are you going to give him up to the law?"

"No," I said, "I believe that this will be a lesson to him. I shall keep an eye on him, of course, for that is but right; but if he stops where he is and reforms, it shall never be said that I betrayed him."

"How good you are!"

"Well, I try to be. It is all a person can do in a world like this."

And now, my burden being shifted to other shoulders, my terrors soon faded away.

—Life on the Mississippi

28. Remedies

Tom's fearful secret and guilty conscience begin to fade in importance as he worries about Becky Thatcher. She is ill, and, for all he tries, he cannot forget her. "The charm of life was gone; here was nothing but dreariness left."

He put his hoop away, and his bat; there was no joy in them any more. His aunt was concerned. She began to try all manner of remedies on him. She was one of those people who are infatuated with . . . all newfangled methods of producing health or mending it . . . . The water treatment was new, now, and Tom's low condition was a windfall to her. She had him out at daylight every morning, stood him up in the woodshed and drowned him with a deluge of cold water. . . .

—Tom Sawyer, **chapter 12**

I was always told that I was a sickly and precarious and tiresome and uncertain child, and lived mainly on allopathic medicines during the first seven years of my life. I asked my mother about this, in her old age—she was in her eighty-eighth year—and said:

"I suppose that during all that time you were uneasy about me?"

"Yes, the whole time."

"Afraid I wouldn't live?"

After a reflective pause—ostensibly to think out the facts—"No—afraid you would."

—Autobiography, Vol. I

I was the subject of my mother's experiment. She was wise. She made experiments cautiously. She didn't pick out just any child in the flock. No, she chose judiciously. She chose one she could spare, and she couldn't spare the others. I was the choice child of the flock, so I had to take all the experiments.

In 1844, Kneipp filled the world with the wonder of the water cure. Mother wanted to try it, but on sober second thought she put me through. A bucket of ice water was poured over to see the effect. Then I was rubbed down with flannels, a sheet was dipped in the water, and I was put to bed. I perspired so much that mother put a life preserver to bed with me.

—Speech before the Assembly
Committee in Albany, N.Y.,
February 27, 1901

29. The Cat and the Painkiller

Painkiller, "simply fire in a liquid form," breaks up Tom's "indifference."
Using reverse psychology, Tom professes to like Painkiller and requests it so often
that Aunt Polly allows him to take it unsupervised. While Tom is pouring it into a
crack in the floor, the cat begs for a taste. Tom obliges him. Aunt Polly enters just
in time to see the cat's wild reaction, and she quickly understands what has
transpired.

The handle of the telltale spoon was visible under the bed valance.
Aunt Polly took it, held it up. Tom winced, and dropped his eyes.
Aunt Polly raised him up by the usual handle—his ear—and cracked
his head soundly with her thimble.

"Now, sir, what did you want to treat that poor dumb beast so
for?"

—Tom Sawyer, **chapter 12**

That sort of interference in behalf of abused animals was a common thing with
her [Jane Clemens'] life . . . . All the race of dumb animals had a friend in her. By
some subtle sign the homeless, hunted, bedraggled, and disreputable cat recognized
her at a glance as the born refuge and champion of his sort—and followed her home.
His instinct was right, and he was as welcome as the prodigal son. We had nineteen
cats at one time, in 1845. And there wasn't one in the lot that had any character, not
one that had any merit, except that cheap and tawdry merit of being unfortunate.
They were a burden to us all—including my mother—but they were out of luck, and
that was enough; they had to stay. However, better these than no pets at all; children
must have pets, and we were not allowed to have caged ones. An imprisoned
creature was out of the question—my mother would not have allowed a rat to be
restrained of its liberty.

—Autobiography, Vol. I

This is the Mississippi as seen today from Riverview Park north of Hannibal. Photograph by Deborah Rush Evans.

30. Searching the River

Tom goes to school and his low condition reverses when he sees Becky Thatcher returning after her long illness. He shows off for her but she scorns him. Crestfallen, Tom gathers his gang, Huck and Joe Harper, and they run off to become pirates. On Jackson's Island, they fish, feast, swim, and play. Then, while resting, they become "dully conscious of a peculiar sound in the distance." They investigate and look out across the wide Mississippi.

There were a great many skiffs rowing about or floating with the stream in the neighborhood of the ferryboat, but the boys could not determine what the men in them were doing. Presently a great jet of white smoke burst from the ferryboat's side, and as it expanded and rose in a lazy cloud, that same dull throb of sound was borne to the listeners again.

"I know now!" exclaimed Tom; "somebody's drownded!"

. . . .

The boys still listened and watched. Presently a revealing thought flashed through Tom's mind, and he exclaimed:

"Boys, I know who's drownded—it's us!"

—Tom Sawyer, **chapter 14**

In his notes for his autobiography, Twain recorded: "Fired cannon to raise drowned bodies of Christ [Clint?] Levering and me—when I escaped from the ferryboat." In the following excerpt from a letter to Will Bowen, Twain reveals some of the details behind his own mistaken drowning which obviously found its way into Tom Sawyer. *(MT&HF)*

I jumped overboard from the ferry boat in the middle of the river that stormy day to get my hat, and swam two or three miles after it (and *got* it) while all the town collected on the wharf and for an hour or so looked out across the angry waste of 'white caps' toward where people said Sam. Clemens was last seen before he went down . . . .

—Letter to Will Bowen (SCH)
February 6, 1870

31. Smoking

Tom sneaks home with the intention of telling his aunt that he hasn't drowned, but changes his mind as he eavesdrops on a conversation between Polly and Mrs. Harper. He is struck by the idea of attending his own funeral.

When he returns to the island, he finds that the boys are becoming homesick. They are just about to go home when Tom unfolds his great secret. They have renewed enthusiasm for pirating, and Tom and Joe ask Huck to teach them to smoke.

Now they stretched themselves out on their elbows and began to puff, charily, and with slender confidence. The smoke had an unpleasant taste, and they gagged a little, but Tom said:

"Why it's just as easy! If I'd 'a' knowed *this* was all, I'd 'a' learnt long ago."

—*Tom Sawyer,* **chapter 16**

I have made it a rule never to smoke more than one cigar at a time. I have no other restriction as regards smoking. I do not know just when I began to smoke, I only know that it was in my father's lifetime, and that I was discreet. He passed from this life early in 1847, when I was a shade past eleven; ever since then I have smoked publicly. As an example to others, and not that I care for moderation myself, it has always been my rule never to smoke when asleep, and never to refrain when awake. It is a good rule. I mean, for me; but some of you know quite well that it wouldn't answer for everybody that's trying to get to be seventy.

I smoke in bed until I have to go to sleep; I wake I up in the night, sometimes once, sometimes twice, sometimes three times and I never waste any of these opportunities to smoke.

—Speech at Delmonico's
Dec. 5, 1905 celebrating his
seventieth birthday

Henry Clemens died when the Pennsylvania, a riverboat of this construction, exploded at Ship Island. Courtesy The Public Library of Cincinnati and Hamilton County.

32. Dream Prophecies

The boys cause a great stir when they appear at their own funeral. Later, when the excitement dies, Aunt Polly scolds Tom for making her suffer so they could have their "fine joke." In a desperate attempt to redeem himself, Tom explains that he does care, and that he dreamt about her at least. When Polly asks about the dream, Tom amazes her with an accurate account of the conversation he overheard.

"Tom! The sperrit was upon you! You was a-prophesying—that's what you was doing! Land alive, go on, Tom!"

—*Tom Sawyer*, **chapter 18**

Mark Twain had a prophetic dream that he did not publish until after the death of his mother. He was afraid the subject would distress her, for it dealt with the death of Twain's brother Henry.

The date of my memorable dream was about the beginning of May, 1858. It was a remarkable dream . . . so vivid, so like reality, that it deceived me, and I thought is *was* real. In the dream I had seen Henry a corpse. He lay in a metallic burial case. He was dressed in a suit of my clothing, and on his breast lay a great bouquet of flowers, mainly white roses, with a red rose in the center. The casket stood upon a couple of chairs. I dressed, and moved toward that door, thinking I would go in there and look at it, but I changed my mind. I thought I could not yet bear to meet my mother. I thought I would wait awhile and make some preparation for that ordeal. The house was on Locust Street, a little above Thirteenth, and I walked to Fourteenth and to the middle of the block beyond before it suddenly flashed upon me that there was nothing real about this—it was only a dream. I can still feel something of the grateful upheaval of joy of that moment, and I can also still feel the remnant of doubt, the suspicion that it was real, after all. I returned to the house almost on a run, flew up the stairs two or three at a jump, and rushed into that sitting room, and was made glad again, for there was no casket there.

(Mark Twain and his brother Henry worked together aboard the riverboat
Pennsylvania. Twain was the pilot's apprentice and his brother was a "mud" clerk,
an unpaid position aboard the ship. The pilot was a cantankerous, vindictive man
who found fault with everything. Mr. Brown was angry at Henry and was about to
hit him with a lump of coal when Mark Twain came to his brother's aid. He struck
the pilot of the riverboat with a heavy stool. He had committed "the crime of
crimes": he had lifted his hand against a pilot on duty. Twain was put ashore in New
Orleans.)

In New Orleans I always had a job. It was my privilege to watch the freight piles
from seven in the evening until seven in the morning . . . . Henry always joined my
watch about nine in the evening, when his own duties were ended, and we often
walked my rounds and chatted together until midnight. This time we were to part,
and so the night before the boat sailed I gave Henry some advice. I said: "In case of
a disaster to the boat, don't lose your head—leave that unwisdom to the
passengers—they are competent—they'll attend to it. . . . "

Two or three days afterward the boat's boilers exploded at Ship Island, below
Memphis, early one morning . . . . I followed the Pennsylvania about a day later, on
another boat, and we began to get news of the disaster at every port we touched at,
and so by the time we reached Memphis we knew all about it.

I found Henry stretched upon a mattress on the floor of a great building, along
with thirty or forty other scalded and wounded persons, and was promptly informed,
by some indiscreet person, that he had inhaled steam, that his body was badly
scalded, and that he would live but a little while . . . . I think he died about dawn, I
don't remember as to that. He was carried to the dead-room and I went away for a
while to a citizen's house and slept off some of my accumulated fatigue—and
meantime something was happening. The coffins provided for the dead were of
unpainted white pine, but in this instance some of the ladies of Memphis had made up
a fund of sixty dollars and bought a metallic case, and when I came back and entered
the dead-room Henry lay in that open case, and he was dressed in a suit of my
clothing. I recognized instantly that my dream of several weeks before was here
exactly reproduced, so far as these details went—and I think I missed one detail, but
that one was immediately supplied, for just then an elderly lady entered the place with

a large bouquet consisting mainly of white roses, and in the center of it was a red rose, and she laid it on his breast.

—*Autobiography,* Vol. I

Will Bowen, Twain's boyhood friend, served as one of the models for the character Tom Sawyer. Courtesy Mark Twain Project, The Bancroft Library.

33. Sentimental Compositions

After his appearance at his own funeral, Tom is now a hero and the envy of all the boys, but Becky is not impressed. She excludes Tom from a picnic she is planning but forgives him when he steps forward and takes her punishment for tearing Mr. Dobbin's book. The school year ends with "examination day," during which students recite lessons and read poetry and original compositions.

A prevalent feature of these compositions was a nursed and petted melancholy; another was a wasteful and opulent gush of "fine language"; and another was a tendency to lug in by the ears particularly prized words and phrases . . . .

—*Tom Sawyer*, chapter 21

During the years when Twain was writing <u>Tom Sawyer</u>, he corresponded with a boyhood friend, Will Bowen, who was his model for Joe Harper. In a letter written to Frank E. Burrough, Twain relates his distaste for the sentimentality that often appeared in Will Bowen's letters. Twain had written to Bowen and told him of his feelings. It is difficult to determine whether Bowen's sentimentality touched off Twain's criticism of sentimental compositions in the above passage or whether the writing of that passage inspired him to confront his friend with his feelings.

There is one thing which I can't stand and *won't* stand, from many people. That is sham sentimentality, the kind a schoolgirl puts into her graduating composition, the sort that makes up the Original Poetry column of a country newspaper, the rot that deals in "the happy days of yore," the "sweet yet melancholy past," with its "blighted hopes" and its "vanished dreams" — and all that sort of drivel.

Will's were always of this stamp. I stood it for years. When I get a letter like that from a grown man and he a widower with a family, it gives me a stomach ache. And I just told Will Bowen so last summer. I told him to stop being 16 at 40, told him to stop drooling about the sweet yet melancholy past, and take a pill.

—Letter to Frank E. Burrough,
Hartford, Conn.
Nov. 1, 1876 (SLMT)

Mark Twain at fifteen proudly displaying his SAM belt buckle.Courtesy Mark
Twain Project, The Bancroft Library.

73

34. Cadets of Temperance

The summer vacation is filled with activity. A circus comes to town, followed by a Negro minstrel show, a phrenologist, and a mesmerizer. Tom is swept up in a temperance movement.

Tom joined the new order of Cadets of Temperance, being attracted by the showy character of their "regalia." He promised to abstain from smoking, chewing, and profanity as long as he remained a member.

—Tom Sawyer, **chapter 22**

In Hannibal, when I was about fifteen, I was for a short time a Cadet of Temperance, an organization which probably covered the whole United States during as much as a year possibly even longer. It consisted in a pledge to refrain, during membership, from the use of tobacco; I mean it consisted partly in that pledge and partly in a red merino sash, but the red merino sash was the main part. The boys joined in order to be privileged to wear it—the pledge part of the matter was of no consequence. It was so small in importance that, contrasted with the sash, it was, in effect, nonexistent. The organization was weak and impermanent because there were not enough holidays to support it. We could turn out and march and show the red sashes—on May Day with the Sunday schools, and on the Fourth of July with the Sunday schools, the independent fire company, and the militia company. But you can't keep a juvenile moral institution alive on two displays of its sash per year. As a private, I could not have held out beyond one procession, but I was Illustrious Grand Worthy Secretary and Royal Inside Sentinel, and had the privilege of inventing the passwords and of wearing a rosette on my sash. Under these conditions, I was enabled to remain steadfast until I had gathered the glory of two displays—May Day and the Fourth of July. Then I resigned straightway, and straightway left the lodge.

—Autobiography, Vol.II

35. Measles

Tom's vacation begins to "hang a little heavy on his hands." Neither minstrel shows nor the circus can distract Tom from the "chronic misery" of his secret.

Then came the measles.
During two long weeks Tom lay a prisoner, dead to the world and its happenings. He was very ill, he was interested in nothing.

—Tom Sawyer, **chapter 22**

When I was twelve and a half years old, my father died. It was in the spring. The summer came, and brought with it an epidemic of measles. For a time, a child died almost every day. The village was paralyzed with fright, distress, despair. Children that were not smitten with the disease were imprisoned in their homes to save them from the infection. In the homes there were no cheerful faces, there was no music, there was no singing but of solemn hymns, no voice but of prayer, no romping was allowed, no noise, no laughter, the family moved spectrally about on tiptoe, in a ghostly hush. I was a prisoner. My soul was steeped in this awful dreariness—and in fear. At some time or other every day and every night a sudden shiver shook me to the marrow, and I said to myself, "There, I've got it! and I shall die." Life on these miserable terms was not worth living, and at last I made up my mind to get the disease and have it over, one way or the other. I escaped from the house and went to the house of a neighbor where a playmate of mine [Will Bowen] was very ill with the malady. When the chance offered I crept into his room and got into bed with him. I was discovered by his mother and sent back into captivity. But I had the disease; they could not take that from me. I came near to dying. The whole village was interested, and anxious, and sent for news of me every day; and not only once, but several times. Everybody believed I would die; but on the fourteenth day a change came for the worse, and they were disappointed.

—The Turning Point of My Life

36. Thoroughly Damned

When Tom recovers from the measles, he discovers that everyone else, including Huck, "has got religion." He feels that he alone of all the town is "lost, forever and forever."

And that night there came a terrific storm, with driving rain, awful claps of thunder, and blinding sheets of lightning. He covered his head with the bedclothes and waited in a horror of suspense for his doom; for he had not the shadow of a doubt that all this hubbub was about him. He believed he had taxed the forbearance of the powers above to the extremity of endurance and that this was the result.

— Tom Sawyer, **chapter 22**

Two of Twain's boyhood acquaintances, Clint Levering and a German lad nicknamed Dutchy, drowned within the space of three weeks. According to his account in Life on the Mississippi, *Clint (fictitiously renamed Lem Hackett) was drowned on a Sunday[3], and a thunderstorm struck that same evening. Mark Twain was convinced, as he tried unsuccessfully to sleep, that this storm was a sign from above and that the heavens were out to get him. He suffered a night of anguish in which he repented and swore to change his ways. In the morning, when the storm had cleared and the sun came out, Mark sensed that perhaps the storm had been a false alarm. He quickly slipped back to his old, sinful ways. Then, three weeks later, Dutchy, who had just recited three thousand verses of scripture, drowned. And then another ferocious storm hit Hannibal.*

That storm came about three weeks later; and it was the most unaccountable one, to me, that I had ever experienced; for on the afternoon of that day, "Dutchy" was drowned.

[3]According to records, Clint Levering died on Friday, August 13, 1947. (SCH)

Circumstances gave to his death a peculiar impressiveness. We were all bathing in a muddy creek which had a deep hole in it, and in this hole the coopers had sunk a pile of green hickory hoop-poles to soak, some twelve feet under water. We were diving and "seeing who could stay under longest." We managed to remain down by holding on to the hoop-poles. Dutchy made such a poor success of it that he was hailed with laughter and derision every time his head appeared above water. At last he seemed hurt with the taunts, and begged us to stand still on the bank and be fair with him and give him an honest count—"be friendly and kind just this once, and not miscount for the sake of having the fun of laughing at him." Treacherous winks were exchanged, and all said, "All right, Dutchy—go ahead, we'll play fair."

Dutchy plunged in, but the boys, instead of beginning to count, followed the lead of one of their number and scampered to a range of blackberry bushes close by and hid behind it. They imagined Dutchy's humiliation, when he should rise after a superhuman effort and find the place silent and vacant, nobody there to applaud. They were "so full of laugh" with the idea that they were continually exploding into muffled cackles. Time swept on, and presently one who was peeping through the briers said, with surprise:

"Why, he hasn't come up yet !"

The laughing stopped.

"Boys, it's a splendid dive," said one.

"Never mind that," said another, "the joke on him is all the better for it."

There was a remark or two more, and then a pause. Talking ceased, and all began to peer through the vines. Before long, the boys' faces began to look uneasy, then anxious, then terrified. Still there was no movement of the placid water. Hearts began to beat fast, and faces to turn pale. We all glided out silently, and stood on the bank, our horrified eyes wandering back and forth from each other's countenances to the water.

"Somebody must go down and see!"

Yes, that was plain; but nobody wanted the grisly task.

"Draw straws!"

So we did—with hands which shook so that we hardly knew what we were about. The lot fell to me, and I went down. The water was so muddy I could not see anything, but I felt around among the hoop-poles, and presently grasped a limp wrist which gave me no response—and if it had I should not have known it, I let it go with such a frightened suddenness.

The boy had been caught among the hoop-poles and entangled there, helplessly.

I fled to the surface and told the awful news. Some of us knew that if the boy were dragged out at once he might possibly be resuscitated, but we never thought of that.

We did not think of anything; we did not know what to do, so we did nothing except that the smaller lads cried piteously, and we all struggled frantically into our clothes, putting on anybody's that came handy, and getting them wrong side out and upside down, as a rule. Then we scurried away and gave the alarm, but none of us went back to see the end of the tragedy. We had a more important thing to attend to: we all flew home, and lost not a moment in getting ready to lead a better life.

The night presently closed down. Then came on that tremendous and utterly unaccountable storm. I was perfectly dazed; I could not understand it. It seemed to me that there must be some mistake. The elements were turned loose, and they rattled and banged in the most blind and frantic manner. All heart and hope went out of me, and the dismal thought kept floating through my brain, "If a boy who knows three thousand verses by heart is not satisfactory, what chance is there for anybody else?"

—*Life on the Mississippi*

John Briggs was one of Twain's boyhood friends. He became Joe Harper in *The Adventures of Tom Sawyer*. Courtesy Mark Twain Project, The Bancroft Library.

37. Real Treasure

Muff Potter's trial arrives, and Tom becomes "a glittering hero once more" when he testifies against Injun Joe. Joe's escape from the courtroom casts a shadow over Tom's exultation. Time passes, and the likelihood of Injun Joe returning for revenge seems remote. Tom's life returns to normal, and he resumes his boyish activities.

There comes a time in every rightly constructed boy's life when he has a raging desire to go somewhere and dig for hidden treasure.

— *Tom Sawyer*, **chapter 25**

In his biography of Mark Twain, Albert Bigelow Paine relates an incident concerning some French trappers who were camped two miles above Hannibal. Their camp was raided by Indians who scalped and killed all the trappers except for one who was out hunting. The Indians overlooked their gold which was buried in a chest near the camp. The surviving trapper fled to Illinois where he told of the massacre and the buried gold. He died before he could return to the camp, but the legend of the gold tantalized local treasure hunters.

Two of those local treasure hunters would later turn up in <u>The Adventures of Tom Sawyer</u>. *Tom Blankenship had a dream about the location of the treasure and offered to share it with John Briggs and Mark Twain if they would help him dig. They dug for two days in the heat of August and then gave up for other recreations.* (MTB)

The California Gold Rush of 1849 also stimulated the imagination of the boys of Hannibal as Mark Twain recounts in the following passage:

In 1849, when the gold-seekers were streaming through our little town of Hannibal, many of our grown men got the gold fever, and I think that all the boys had it. On the Saturday holidays in summertime we used to borrow skiffs whose owners were not present and go down the river three miles to the cave hollow, and there we staked out claims and pretended to dig gold, panning out half a dollar a day at first; two or three times as much, later, and by and by whole fortunes, as our imaginations became inured to the work. Stupid and unprophetic lads! We were doing this in play and never suspecting. Why, that cave hollow and all the adjacent hills were made of gold ! — but we did not know it. We took it for dirt. We left its rich secret in its own peaceful possession and grew up in poverty and want wandering about the world struggling for bread—and this because we had not the gift of prophecy. That region was all dirt and rocks to us, yet all it needed was to be ground up and scientifically handled and it was gold. That is to say, the whole region was a cement mine—and they make the finest kind of Portland cement there now, five thousand barrels a day, with a plant that cost $2,000,000.

—*Autobiography*, Vol. II

38. A Gang of Robbers

After digging for treasure under "dead-limb trees," Tom and Huck agree to try
the haunted house. While Tom and Huck are exploring upstairs, Injun Joe and his
partner enter the house. The men decide to bury their small bag of coins for safe
keeping and in doing so discover a treasure box already buried in the same location.

The box was soon unearthed. It was not very large; it was iron
bound and had been very strong before the slow years had injured it.
The men contemplated the treasure awhile in blissful silence.

"Pard, there's thousands of dollars here," said Injun Joe.

"'Twas always said that Murrel's gang used to be around here one
summer," the stranger observed.

— Tom Sawyer, **chapter 26**

John A. Murel had an extensive network of confederates who planned and
executed all manner of crimes. He often traveled disguised as an itinerant preacher
whose sermons were so moving that the listeners would not notice that their horses
were being stolen. He would also talk slaves into escaping from their masters to
become partners with him. The slave would agree to be sold to another master for a
percentage of the profit. Then he would escape and be sold again. After being sold
three or four times, the slave was usually murdered, for he was the only witness
against the gang. Murel's most ambitious plan was to organize a revolt among
slaves in New Orleans so that he could gain control of the territory.

Twain remembered Murel's gang when he traveled the Mississippi to get
material for Life on the Mississippi. *As the steamer Gold Dust passed landmarks*
that were familiar to him in his piloting days, Twain noted one island in particular:

There is a tradition that Island 37 was one of the principal abiding places of the
once celebrated "Murel's gang." This was a colossal combination of robbers, horse-

thieves, negro-stealers, and counterfeiters, engaged in business along the river some fifty or sixty years ago. While our journey across the country toward St. Louis was in progress we had had no end of Jesse James and his stirring history; for he had just been assassinated by an agent of the Government of Missouri, and was in consequence occupying a good deal of space in the newspapers. Cheap histories of him were for sale by train-boys. According to these, he was the most marvelous creature of his kind that ever existed. It was a mistake. Murel was his equal in boldness, in pluck, in rapacity; in cruelty, brutality, heartlessness, treachery, and in general and comprehensive vileness and shamelessness; and very much his superior in some larger aspects. James was a retail rascal; Murel, wholesale. James's modest genius dreamed of no loftier flight than the planning of raids upon cars, coaches, and country banks. Murel projected negro insurrections and the capture of New Orleans; and furthermore, on occasion, this Murel could go into a pulpit and edify the congregation. What are James and his half-dozen vulgar rascals compared with this stately old-time criminal, with his sermons, his meditated insurrections and city-captures, and his majestic following of ten hundred men, sworn to do his evil will!

—Life on the Mississippi

39. A Body on the Floor

Fearing that the treasure will be found by someone else, Joe decides to hide it at his "Number Two." Tom and Huck agree to "track the money" and conclude that "Number Two" must be a room in a tavern. Several nights later, using some of Aunt Polly's keys, Tom gets an opportunity to sneak into room #2 of the Temperance Tavern while Huck stands watch in an alley. After an interminable wait, Huck is passed by Tom who yells, "Run for your life!" Later Tom explains:

" . . . I took hold of the knob, and open comes the door! It warn't locked! I hopped in, and shook off the towel, and, great Caesar's ghost! . . . I most stepped on Injun Joe's hand!"

—*Tom Sawyer*, **chapter 28**

It is hard to forget repulsive things. I remember yet how I ran off from school once, when I was a boy, and then, pretty late at night, concluded to climb into the window of my father's office and sleep on a lounge, because I had a delicacy about going home and getting thrashed. As I lay on the lounge and my eyes grew accustomed to the darkness, I fancied I could see a long, dusky, shapeless thing stretched upon the floor. A cold shiver went through me. I turned my face to the wall. That did not answer. I was afraid that that thing would creep over and seize me in the dark. I turned back and stared at it for minutes and minutes—they seemed hours. It appeared to me that the lagging moonlight never, never would get to it. I turned to the wall and counted fifty—it was almost touching it. With desperate will I turned again and counted one hundred, and faced about, all in a tremble. A white human hand lay in the moonlight! Such an awful sinking at the heart—such a gasp for breath! I felt—I cannot tell *what* I felt. When I recovered strength enough, I faced the wall again. But no boy could have remained so, with that mysterious hand behind him. I counted again, and looked—the most of a naked arm was exposed. I put my hands over my eyes and counted till I could stand it no longer, and then—the pallid face of a man was there, with the corners of his mouth drawn down, and the eyes fixed and glassy in death! I raised to a sitting posture and glowered on that corpse till the light crept down the bare breast,—line by line—inch by inch . . . and then it disclosed a ghastly stab!

I went away from there. I do not say that I went away in any sort of a hurry, but I simply went—that is sufficient. I went out at the window, and I carried the sash along with me. I did not need the sash, but it was handier to take it than to leave it, and so I took it. I was not scared, but I was considerably agitated.

When I reached home, they whipped me, but I enjoyed it. It seemed perfectly delightful. That man had been stabbed near the office that afternoon, and they carried him in there to doctor him, but he lived for only an hour. I have slept in the same room with him often, since then—in my dreams.

—The Innocents Abroad, Vol. I

John Clemens's law office, just below the Hawkins's residence, was the scene of Twain's memorable night. Photograph by Deborah Rush Evans.

40. The Widow Douglas

Huck agrees to watch the tavern every night for another opportunity if Tom promises to be the one to enter the room. However, when Becky returns from Constantinople, and the date for the "long-promised" picnic is set, Tom pushes thoughts of Huck and the treasure aside.

After the picnic, Becky is supposed to spend the night with the Harpers, but Tom has other plans.

Presently as they tripped along, Tom said to Becky:

"Say—I'll tell you what we'll do. 'Stead of going to Joe Harper's we'll climb right up the hill and stop at the Widow Douglas's. She'll have ice cream! She has it most every day—dead loads of it. And she'll be awful glad to have us."

—*Tom Sawyer,* chapter 29

In 1897, while in Switzerland, Mark Twain wrote a manuscript entitled <u>Villagers of 1840-3</u> *in which he catalogued, from memory, brief and sketchy biographies of the inhabitants of Hannibal, Missouri. Among them was Mrs. Richard Holiday.* (HHT)

Mrs. Holiday. Was a MacDonald, born Scotch. Wore her father's ivory miniature—a British General in the Revolution. Lived on Holiday's Hill. Well off. Hospitable. Fond of having parties of young people. Widow. Old, but anxious to marry. Always consulting fortune-tellers; always managed to make them understand that she had been promised 3 by the first fraud. They always confirmed the prophecy. She finally died before the prophecies had a full chance.

—*Villagers of 1840-3* (HHT)

McDowell's Cave, located in Cave Hollow a mile south of Hannibal, was one of Twain's favorite places. The original entrance to the cave is above and to the left of this entrance which was excavated into the hillside for easier access. Courtesy the Mark Twain Museum.

41. Caves

At "Cave Hollow," the picnickers work up responsible appetites. After eating, someone suggests entering McDougal's cave. Candles are procured, and everyone scampers up the hillside to the cave entrance.

. . . McDougal's Cave was but a vast labyrinth of crooked aisles that ran into each other and out again and led nowhere. It was said that one might wander days and nights . . . and never find the end of the cave.

— *Tom Sawyer,* **chapter 29**

Many excursion parties came from considerable distances up and down the river to visit the cave. It was miles in extent and was a tangled wilderness of narrow and lofty clefts and passages. It was an easy place to get lost in; anybody could do it—including the bats. I got lost in it myself, along with a lady, and our last candle burned down to almost nothing before we glimpsed the search party's lights winding about in the distance.

. . . .

The cave was an uncanny place, for it contained a corpse—the corpse of a young girl of fourteen. It was in a glass cylinder inclosed in a copper one which was suspended from a rail which bridged a narrow passage.[4] The body was preserved in alcohol, and it was said that loafers and rowdies used to drag it up by the hair and look at the dead face. The girl was the daughter of a St. Louis surgeon [Dr. Joseph Nash McDowell] of extraordinary ability and wide celebrity. He was an eccentric man and did many strange things. He put the poor thing in that forlorn place himself.

—*Autobiography,* Vol. I

[4]It is thought that Dr. McDowell was experimenting to see if a human body would petrify.

The Welshman's house was restored and moved to its present site in 1961.
Photograph by Deborah Rush Evans.

42. A Widow Saved

While Tom is enjoying the picnic, Huck remains faithful to his task, and that night he sees two men leaving the tavern with a box. Huck follows them to the Widow Douglas's grounds.

A deadly chill went to Huck's heart—this, then, was the "revenge" job! His thought was to fly. Then he remembered that the Widow Douglas had been kind to him more than once, and maybe they were going to murder her.

— *Tom Sawyer*, **chapter 29**

Then there was the case of the young California emigrant who got drunk and proposed to raid the "Welshman's house" all alone one dark and threatening night. This house stood halfway up Holliday's Hill and its sole occupants were a poor but quite respectable widow and her blameless daughter. The invading ruffian woke the whole village with his ribald yells and course challenges and obscenities. I went up there with a comrade—John Briggs, I think—to look and listen. The figure of the man was dimly visible; the women were on their porch, not visible in the deep shadow of its roof, but we heard the elder woman's voice. She loaded an old musket with slugs, and she warned the man that if he stayed where he was while she counted ten it would cost him his life. She began to count, slowly; he began to laugh. He stopped laughing at "six"; then through the deep stillness, in a steady voice, followed the rest of the tale: "Seven . . . eight . . . nine" — a long pause, we holding our breaths—"ten!" A red spout of flame gushed out into the night, and the man dropped with his breast riddled to rags. Then the rain and the thunder burst loose and the waiting town swarmed up the hill in the glare of the lightning like an invasion of ants. Those people saw the rest; I had had my share and was satisfied. I went home to dream, and was not disappointed.

— *Autobiography*, Vol. I

43. Bats

While Huck is busy rescuing the Widow, Tom and Becky are still in McDougal's Cave. Awed by the natural wonders they encounter, they drift into unexplored regions of the cave.

Under the roof vast knots of bats had packed themselves together, thousands in a bunch; the lights disturbed the creatures, and they came flocking down by the hundreds, squeaking and darting furiously at the candles.

—*Tom Sawyer*, **chapter 31**

A bat is beautifully soft and silky; I do not know any creature that is pleasanter to the touch or is more grateful for caressings, if offered in the right spirit. I know all about these coleoptera, because our great cave, three miles below Hannibal, was multitudinously stocked with them, and often I brought them home to amuse my mother with. It was easy to manage if it was a school day, because then I had ostensibly been to school and hadn't any bats. She was not a suspicious person, but full of trust and confidence; and when I said, "There's something in my coat pocket for you," she would put her hand in. But she always took it out again, herself; I didn't have to tell her. It was remarkable, the way she couldn't learn to like private bats. The more experience she had, the more she could not change her views.

—*Autobiography*, Vol. I

McDowell's Cave, like McDougal's cave in *The Adventures of Tom Sawyer*, was "a vast labyrinth of crooked aisles." Photograph by Deborah Rush Evans.

44. Lost in a Cave

Tom and Becky escape from the bats and get lost in the cave. When their food and candles are used up, Tom explores some side passages and runs into Injun Joe, who flees. In a last effort to find a way out, Tom, anchored to a kite line, again explores. This time he sees "a speck of daylight." Later, at Judge Thatcher's house, Tom relates his experience:

He told how he went back for Becky; . . . how he pushed his way out at the hole; . . . how some men came along in a skiff and . . . didn't believe the wild tale . . . "because," they said, "you are five miles down the river below the valley the cave is in . . . ."

— Tom Sawyer, **chapter 32**

"General" Gaines, who was our first town drunkard before Jimmy Finn got the place, was lost in there [the cave] for the space of a week, and finally pushed his handkerchief out of a hole in a hilltop near Saverton, several miles down the river from the cave's mouth, and somebody saw it and dug him out. There is nothing the matter with his statistics except the handkerchief. I knew him for years and he hadn't any. But it could have been his nose. That would attract attention.

—Autobiography, Vol. I

45. The Death of Injun Joe

Two weeks after his rescue, Tom stops to visit Becky and learns from her father that the cave door has been "sheathed with boiler iron." Tom is horrified and exclaims, "Oh, judge, Injun Joe's in the cave!"

When the cave door was unlocked, a sorrowful sight presented itself . . . . Injun Joe lay stretched upon the ground dead . . . . He had also contrived to catch a few bats, and these . . . he had eaten, leaving only their claws. The poor unfortunate had starved to death.

—Tom Sawyer, **chapter 33**

"Injun Joe," the half-breed, got lost in there once, and would have starved to death if the bats had run short. But there was no chance of that; there were myriads of them. He told me all his story. In the book called *Tom Sawyer* I starved him entirely to death in the cave, but that was in the interest of art; it never happened.

—Autobiography, Vol. I

46. A Stolen Skiff

Having seen Injun Joe in the cave, Tom realizes that the cave must be the "Number Two" where the treasure is hidden. Tom and Huck gather the equipment necessary to re-enter the cave.

A trifle after noon the boys borrowed a small skiff from a citizen who was absent, and got underway at once.

— *Tom Sawyer,* chapter 33

. . . I met in that town of Hannibal a schoolmate of mine, John Briggs, whom I had not seen for more than fifty years . . . . We spent a whole afternoon going about here and there and yonder, and hunting up the scenes and talking of the crimes which we had committed so long ago . . . . John said, "Can you point out the place where Bear Creek used to be before the railroad came?" I said, "Yes, it ran along yonder." And can you point out the swimming hole?" "Yes, out there." And he said, "Can you point out the place where we stole the skiff?" Well, I didn't know which one he meant. Such a wilderness of events had intervened since that day, more than fifty years ago, it took me more than five minutes to call back that little incident, and then I did call it back; it was a white skiff, and we painted it red to allay suspicion. And the saddest, saddest man came along—a stranger he was—and he looked that red skiff over so pathetically, and he said: "Well, if it weren't for its complexion I'd know whose skiff that was." He said it in that pleading way, you know, that appeals for sympathy and suggestion; we were full of sympathy for him, but we weren't in any condition to offer suggestions. I can see him yet as he turned away with that same sad look on his face and vanished out of history forever. I wonder what became of that man. I know what became of the skiff.

—Speech at the Metropolitan Club
New York, New York
November 28, 1902

47. The End of a Chronicle

Most of the characters that perform in this book still live, and are prosperous and happy. Some day it may seem worth while to take up the story of the younger ones again and see what sort of men and women they turned out to be . . . .

—Tom Sawyer, conclusion

Mark Twain never did take up the story of his younger ones and follow them into adulthood. He did have Huckleberry Finn continue his story after escaping once again from society. Becky Thatcher surfaces in this story as Bessie Thatcher, Tom Sawyer makes an appearance, and there is even mention of Sid. Tom travels abroad in one sequel and plays detective in another, but we are never to learn what becomes of them as adults.

The children of Mark Twain's Hannibal who became the characters in Tom Sawyer *grew up and went their separate ways. In 1882, Mark Twain returned briefly to Hannibal, Missouri, gathering material for* Life on the Mississippi.

In a letter to his wife, Livy, written in May of that year, Twain discusses his return to Hannibal:

I have spent three delightful days in Hannibal, loitering around all day long, examining the old localities and talking with the greyheads who were boys and girls with me 30 or 40 years ago. It has been a moving time . . . . That world which I knew in its blossoming youth is old and bowed and melancholy now. Its soft cheeks are leathery and wrinkled. The fire is gone out in its eyes and the spring from its step. It will be dust and ashes when I come again.

—Letter to Livy, Hartford
Quincy, Ill.
May 17, 1882

Twain made references to those boys and girls in his autobiography, and briefly revealed "what sort of men and women they turned out to be."

Huck Finn: (Tom Blankenship)

... I heard, four years ago, that he was justice of the peace in a remote village in Montana, and was a good citizen and greatly respected.

—*Autobiography,* Vol. II

Joe Harper: (John Briggs)

John Briggs. Worked as a stemmer in Garth's [tobacco] factory. Became a 6-footer and a capable rebel private.

—*Villagers of 1840-3*

Amy Lawrence: (Artimisia Briggs)

[Artimisia Briggs] . . . got married not long after refusing me. She married Richmond, the stone mason, who was my Methodist Sunday-school teacher in the earliest days . . . .

—*Autobiography,* Vol. II

Willie Mufferson, the model boy: (Theodore Dawson)

. . . I was told what became of him, but as it was a disappointment to me, I will not go into details. He succeeded in life.

—*Life on the Mississippi I*

Becky Thatcher: (Laura Hawkins)

Laura lived to be the mother of six 6-foot sons. Died.

— *Villagers of 1840-3* (HHT)

Twain was incorrect when he assumed that Laura Hawkins Frazer was dead. He met her in Hannibal in 1902 and they dined together. In 1908, she appeared with her granddaughter as a guest at Stormfield, Twain's home in Redding, Connecticut. She died in 1928. (HHT)

Tom Sawyer: (Mark Twain)

In his preface to <u>The Adventures of Tom Sawyer,</u> Twain indicates that the character of Tom is a composite of the characteristics of three boys that he knew. Among those three was Will Bowen, Twain's life-long friend. Like Twain, both he and his brother Sam became riverboat pilots. Undoubtedly, the larger portion of that "composite order of architecture" is Twain.

It is hardly necessary to tell what kind of man the Tom Sawyer of Hannibal turned out to be. In a letter to an unidentified person, Twain gave a brief autobiographical sketch:

I was a soldier two weeks once in the beginning of the war and was hunted like a rat the whole time . . . . I have shoveled silver tailings in a quartz mill a couple of weeks, and acquired the last possibilities of culture in that direction. And I've done "pocket mining" during three months in one little patch of ground in the whole globe where Nature conceals gold in pockets—or did, before we robbed all of those pockets and exhausted, obliterated, annihilated the most curious freak Nature ever indulged in. There are not thirty men left alive who, being told there was a pocket hidden on the broad slope of a mountain, would know how to go find it or have the faintest idea of how to set about it—but I am one of the possible 20 or 30 who possess the secret and I could go and put my hand on that hidden treasure with a most deadly precision.

And I've been a prospector and know pay rock from poor when I find it— just with a touch of the tongue. And I've been a silver miner and know how to dig and shovel and drill, and put in a blast . . . .

And I was a newspaper reporter four years in cities and so saw the inside of many things; and was reporter in a legislature two sessions and the same in Congress one session—and thus learned to know personally three sample-bodies of the smallest minds and the selfishest souls and the cowardliest hearts that God makes.

And I was some years a Mississippi pilot and familiarly knew all the different kinds of steamboatmen—a race apart and not like other folk.

And I was for some years a traveling "jour" printer, and wandered from city to city—and so know that sect familiarly.

And I was a lecturer on the public platform a number of seasons and was a responder to toasts at all the different kinds of banquets—and so I know a great many secrets about audiences—secrets not to be got out of books but only acquirable by experience.

And I watched over one dear project of mine five years, spent a fortune on it, and failed to make it go—and the history of that would make a large book in which a million men would see themselves as in a mirror; and they would testify and say, Verily this is not imagination, this fellow has been there—and after would they cast dust upon their heads, cursing and blaspheming.

And I am a publisher and did pay to one author's widow [General Grant's] the largest copyright checks this world has ever seen—aggregating more than L 80,000 in the first year.

And I have been an author for 20 years and an ass for 55.

> —Letter to an unidentified
> person, 1890. (PMT)

And he remains one of America's most beloved writers.

Photograph taken of Mark Twain in 1907. Courtesy Mark
Twain Project, The Bancroft Library.

Unless noted by the following abbreviations, all quotations are taken from *The Complete Works of Mark Twain* (American Artists Edition), 26 vols.New York.

HH&T

Mark Twain's Hannibal, Huck, & Tom, Walter Blair, ed., University of California Press: Berkeley & Los Angeles, 1969.

MTB

Mark Twain: A Biography, Albert Bigelow Paine, Harper & Brothers: New York, 1946.

MTL

Mark Twain's Letters, Volume I (1853-66) & Volume II (1867-68), Harriet Elinor Smith & Richard Bucci, eds., University of California Press: Berkeley, Los Angeles, 1990.

MTN&J

Mark Twain's Notebooks and Journals, Volumes I & II, Frederick Anderson, Lin Salamo, and Bernard L. Stein Eds. University of California Press: Berkeley, Los Angeles, 1975.

PMT

The Portable Mark Twain, Bernard DeVoto, New York: The Viking Press, 1968.

SCH

Sam Clemens of Hannibal, Dixon Wecter, Houghton Mifflin Company: Boston, 1952.

SLMT

The Selected Letters of Mark Twain, Charles Neider, ed., Harper & Row: New York, 1982.

Blair, Walter. *Mark Twain and Huck Finn.* University of California Press: Berkeley, 1960.

Clemens, Samuel L. *Mark Twain's Notebooks and Journals,* Vol. I *(1855-1873).* Edited by Frederick Anderson, Michael B. Frank, and Kenneth M. Sanderson. University of California Press: Berkeley, 1975.

————· *Mark Twain's Hannibal, Huck & Tom.* Edited by Walter Blair. University of California Press: Berkeley, 1969.

————· *Mark Twain's Letters.* 2 vols. Edited by Albert Bigelow Paine. Harper & Brothers: New York, 1927.

————· *Mark Twain's Letters,* Vol. I: *1853-1866.* Edited by Edgar Marquess Branch, Michael B. Frank, Kenneth M. Anderson. University of California Press: Berkeley, 1988.

————· *Mark Twain's Letters,* Vol. II: *1867-1868.* Edited by Harriet Elinor Smith, Lin Salamo, Richard Bucci. University of California Press: Berkeley, 1990.

————· *Mark Twain's Letters to Will Bowen.* Edited by Theodore Hornberger. The University of Texas: Austin, 1941.

————· *The Selected Letters of Mark Twain.* Edited by Charles Neider. Harper & Row: New York, 1982.

————· *The Complete Works of Mark Twain.* American Artists Edition. 26 Vols. Harper and Brothers: New York, n. d.

DeVoto, Bernard. *Mark Twain at Work.* Harvard University Press: Cambridge, 1942.

———· *The Portable Mark Twain.* HarperCollins: New York, 1974.

Emerson, Everett H. *The Authentic Mark Twain: A Literary Biography of Samuel L. Clemens.* University of Pennsylvania Press: Philadelphia, 1984.

Hagood, J. Hurley and Roberta (Roland). *Mirror of Hannibal.* Hannibal Free Public Library, 1990.

Holy Bible, The. Revised Standard Version, Thomas Nelson & Sons: New York, 1953.

Kaplan, Justin. *Mr. Clemens and Mark Twain.* Simon and Schuster: New York, 1966.

Meltzer, Milton. *Mark Twain Himself: A Pictorial Biography.* Bonanza Books: New York, 1960.

"Mark Twain on Training That Pays," *New York Times*, March 17, 1901.

Paine, Albert Bigelow. *Mark Twain, A Biography.* 4 vols. Harper & Brothers: New York, 1912.

Sanborn, Margaret. *Mark Twain: The Bachelor Years.* Doubleday Dell: New York, 1990.

Way, Frederick Jr., comp. *Way's Packet Directory 1848-1983.* Ohio University: Athens, 1983

Wecter, Dixon. *Sam Clemens of Hannibal.* Houghton Mifflin Company: Boston, 1952.

Index

Bold type indicates photograph or illustration.